THE ICE CUBE TREES

tate publishing
CHILDREN'S DIVISION

The Ice Cube Trees
Copyright © 2016 by D. Michael Carriere. All rights reserved.

This title is also available as a Tate Out Loud product. Visit www.tatepublishing.com for more information.

No part of this publication may be reproduced, stored in a retrieval system or transmitted in any way by any means, electronic, mechanical, photocopy, recording or otherwise without the prior permission of the author except as provided by USA copyright law.

The opinions expressed by the author are not necessarily those of Tate Publishing, LLC.

This novel is a work of fiction. Names, descriptions, entities, and incidents included in the story are products of the author's imagination. Any resemblance to actual persons, events, and entities is entirely coincidental.

Published by Tate Publishing & Enterprises, LLC
127 E. Trade Center Terrace | Mustang, Oklahoma 73064 USA
1.888.361.9473 | www.tatepublishing.com

Tate Publishing is committed to excellence in the publishing industry. The company reflects the philosophy established by the founders, based on Psalm 68:11,
"The Lord gave the word and great was the company of those who published it."

Book design copyright © 2016 by Tate Publishing, LLC. All rights reserved.
Cover and interior design by Ralph Lim
Illustrations by Michael Bermundo

Published in the United States of America

ISBN: 978-1-68270-585-8
1. Juvenile Nonfiction / Science & Nature / Discoveries
2. Juvenile Nonfiction / Science & Nature / Flowers & Plants
15.12.11

This book belongs to:

_____

To Kelsey and Emily

Have you ever seen trees growing on top of a very large ice cube? Have you every seen trees wearing winter coats? Could their roots grow in the ice? Could their leaves grow in an ice cube forest? That's impossible, isn't it?

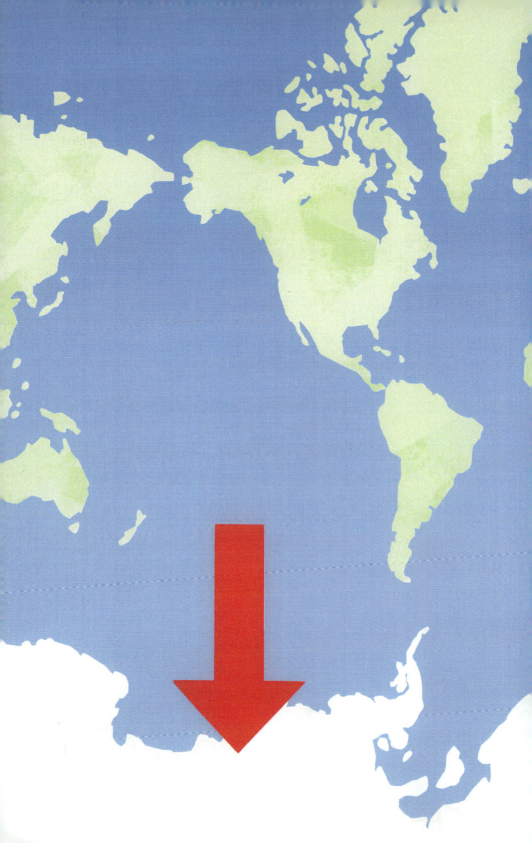

But there is a very cold place called Antarctica. It is one of the seven continents of the world. It's like a giant ice cube with lots of snow on top of it. It's located at the bottom of the world. But it couldn't have been freezing cold all the time. Why? Because trees once grew and lived there at two different times.

But how could anyone know that trees once grew there? Did they dig big holes through the snow and ice and find some trees? No.

But they did drill a hole underwater far below the bottom of the seafloor. And as they looked through the many layers of earth, there was a big surprise.

They found very small parts of trees. They checked to see if they came from other parts of the world. But they did not. They had to have grown in Antarctica.

So let's see who these ice cube trees were. First, there was Miss Conifer. She had lots of needles instead of leaves. She wasn't very tall and was kind of bushy.

Then there was Mr. Southern Beech. He had a very smooth bark, had a lot of leaves, and grew tall. Mr. Beech could also have lived to be very old. A southern beech tree living not far from Antarctica has had over three thousand birthdays.

Perhaps the most surprising discovery of all was that palm trees also grew there. One of the ice cube trees was the tropical palm tree, which probably grew coconuts and figs like they do today.

Just think if those scientists didn't drill that deep hole far underwater. No one would have ever known Miss Conifer, Mr. Southern Beech, or Miss Palm ever lived there. It's always good to learn new things about nature and the different kinds of life on earth. And it's also important for explorers and scientists to keep studying and searching and learning.

Maybe you will be an explorer some day and discover something that no one ever knew existed. Or maybe having an idea and do experiments and uncover a mystery about the earth or one of its many life-forms. You just never know what great event a day can bring if you work hard and keep on searching for the truth.

listen|imagine|view|experience

AUDIO BOOK DOWNLOAD INCLUDED WITH THIS BOOK!

In your hands you hold a complete digital entertainment package. In addition to the paper version, you receive a free download of the audio version of this book. Simply use the code listed below when visiting our website. Once downloaded to your computer, you can listen to the book through your computer's speakers, burn it to an audio CD or save the file to your portable music device (such as Apple's popular iPod) and listen on the go!

How to get your free audio book digital download:

1. Visit www.tatepublishing.com and click on the e|LIVE logo on the home page.
2. Enter the following coupon code:
   3e18-4e77-0336-53ed-680e-6a72-159e-7d69
3. Download the audio book from your e|LIVE digital locker and begin enjoying your new digital entertainment package today!